Contents

Fiction
Fishing for...
page 2

Play
The Lump of Stone
page 22

Poem
What It's Meant To Be
page 28

Non-fiction
Art Surprises
page 30

Written by
David Grant

Illustrated by
Rosy Higgins

Series editor **Dee Reid**

Before reading
Fishing for Trouble

Characters

Keri

Ash

A man and woman

Tricky words

ch1 p4	squealed	ch3 p10	valuable
ch1 p5	spluttering	ch3 p13	whispered
ch2 p8	saucepan	ch3 p14	sculpture
ch2 p10	disappointed	ch4 p17	shrieked

Story starter

Ash and Keri were fishing in the river, by the bridge, when an old scruffy car skidded to a halt on the bridge. They watched as a hand hurled a brown sack out of the car window. The sack sank under the water. Then the car sped off down the road. Ash and Keri decided to find out what was going on.

Fishing for Trouble

Chapter One

Ash and Keri were fishing by the bridge. "This is hopeless," said Ash. "We've been here for three hours and we haven't caught a thing. I don't know why we bother. We never have any luck."

"Today might be our lucky day!"
replied Keri.
"Sure!" said Ash. "I'll believe that when it happens!"
"Sssh!" said Keri. "What's that noise?"
The noise got louder. It was a car and it was moving at speed. It drove onto the bridge, then the brakes squealed and the car skidded to a halt.

The car was old and scruffy. Its engine was spluttering and thick clouds of black smoke were shooting from the exhaust. Ash and Keri watched as one of the front windows slid down. A hand came out of the window holding a brown sack. The hand hurled the sack over the side of the bridge and into the river. The sack landed with a loud splash and sank under the water.

Suddenly the car roared into life again and sped off down the road. Ash looked at Keri.

"What was all that about?" he asked.

"I don't know," said Keri, "but I'm going to find out!"

Chapter Two

"Are you going to dive into the river and pull out that sack?" asked Ash.
Keri laughed.
"No!" she said. "I'm going to fish it out!"
She cast her fishing line into the water and slowly reeled it in.
"Have you got it?" asked Ash.
"No," said Keri. She cast the fishing line out again.

"I've got it!" Keri cried, reeling in the line. "Let's see," said Ash ... but it was only a battered old saucepan.

"Let's go home," sighed Ash. "The sack has probably only got rubbish in it."
"One more try," said Keri, casting out her line.
At once she felt the line go tight.
"I've got something!" she cried.
She reeled in her line and dragged the brown sack out of the river.
"Open it and see what's inside," said Ash.
Quickly, Keri untied the string around the top of the sack and tipped something heavy out onto the bank.

"Oh," said Ash, sounding disappointed. "It's only a lump of stone. Why would someone put *that* in a sack and chuck it in the river?"

"Maybe they weren't really throwing it away," said Keri.

"What do you mean?" asked Ash.

"Maybe the stone is something valuable. I bet they were just hiding it and they will be back to fetch it!" said Keri.

Chapter Three

"The people in that car must have hidden the stone in the river to keep it safe," said Keri. "Let's take it to the police."

"What if the people come back for it?" asked Ash.

"Let's put a different stone in the sack instead and put it in the river," said Keri. "Then we can wait to see if they come back."

Ash and Keri waited … and waited.
It began to get dark but there was a
full moon.

"I'm getting cold and hungry," said Ash,
"and I don't think those people are
coming back."

"Maybe you're right," said Keri. "It's only
a silly old stone. Perhaps we had better
go home."

They were just starting to pack up their stuff when they heard a noise. It was the scruffy old car coming back.
"Hide!" whispered Ash.
Keri and Ash hid behind a bush. The car stopped on the bridge and a man and a woman got out.

"It's dead easy," whispered the man. "We get the sack, we sell the sculpture for loads of money and we'll be rich!"

"What if someone sees us?" said the woman.

"There's no one here," said the man. "Come on!"

"Now what do we do?" whispered Keri.
"I've got an idea," said Ash. "Get your fishing rod ready."
Ash got his phone out of his pocket.
"Who are you calling?" asked Keri.
"The police," said Ash.

Chapter Four

The man and woman walked down to the river bank.

"How are you going to find one little sack in a big river like this?" asked the woman.

"I know where I threw it," said the man. He took off his shoes, rolled up his trousers and started to wade out into the river.

"Ready?" whispered Ash. "You get him. I'll get her, OK?"

Keri nodded.

"Hey!" yelled the man. "What's going on?"
Keri had cast her fishing line and hooked the man's trousers. She started to reel him in.

"Help!" the woman shrieked. "Something is pulling on my coat!"
Ash had cast his fishing line and hooked the woman's coat. He started to reel her in.

Then Keri and Ash ran round and round the man and woman, tying them up in the fishing lines.

"Get this thing off me!" shouted the woman as she struggled to get free. "Let me go!" shouted the man, but his cries were drowned out by the wail of a police siren.

Two police officers jumped out of their car and hurried down to the river bank. Ash and Keri told them what had happened. One police officer inspected the stone carefully.
"That's the sculpture that was stolen from the art gallery this morning!" she said. "It's worth a fortune!"

"Well done, you two," said the other police officer. "You'll be getting a big reward for this."
"You said we never catch anything," said Keri to Ash, "but today we caught two criminals and a big reward!"

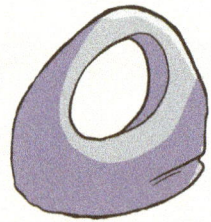

Quiz

Text detective

- **p10** Why is Ash disappointed?
- **p14** What do the thieves plan to do with the sculpture?
- **p16** How can you tell the woman doesn't think much of the man's plan?
- **p20** Explain Keri's joke at the end.

Word detective

- **p5** Which words and phrases tell you that the car is not new?
- **p16** Find a verb that means 'paddle'.
- **p18** Find a word that means a type of loud noise.

What do you think?

Should Ash and Keri have waited by the bridge for the people to return? Should they have phoned the police as soon as they saw the sack thrown into the river? Do you think the thieves had a good plan for hiding the hidden sculpture?

HA! HA!

Q: What is the richest fish in the world?

A: A goldfish!

Before reading
The Lump of Stone

Characters
- **Ash**
- **Keri**
- **Mr Sharp** – their teacher

Setting the scene

Keri and Ash are fishing by the bridge when someone throws a sack into the river. Keri fishes out the sack and inside it they find a lump of stone. Mr Sharp stops to talk to them. He wants to show the stone to the Art teacher at school but Keri has other plans.

The Lump of Stone

Ash: Why would someone put a lump of stone in a sack and throw it in a river?

Keri: I don't know. What do you think it is?

Ash: It just looks like a lump of concrete with a hole in it.

(Mr Sharp is walking his dog on the river bank. He stops to talk to Ash and Keri.)

Mr Sharp: Hello you two. What are you up to?

Ash: We're fishing.

Mr Sharp: Have you caught any fish?

Ash: Well, it's quite funny, really. This car drove past and –

Keri: *(quickly)* No. We haven't caught any fish at all.

Ash: Er, no, not a single one.

Keri: It's like the fish are staying away.

Mr Sharp: Well, never mind. That's a funny looking piece of stone you've got there.

Keri: We just found it. Here, on the river bank.

Ash: No, we didn't! We –

(Keri elbows Ash in the ribs.)

Ash: Oh, yeah, that's right. We just found it.

Keri: It's just a lump of stone.

Ash: What do you think it is?

Mr Sharp: I don't know. But it looks quite interesting. Do you think we should show it to Miss Jones, the Art teacher?

Keri: No! Let's not do that. We need it!

Mr Sharp: You need a lump of stone? Why?

Keri: I want to take it home. My dad would like it. He's doing up our garden. Um … he's making a rockery. He needs loads of stones like this.

Mr Sharp: Oh, all right then. Well, good luck with the fishing.

Keri: Thanks.

Mr Sharp: See you both at school on Monday. Don't be late!

Ash: Yeah, see you.

(Mr Sharp walks off.)

Keri: Phew!

Ash: Why did you tell Mr Sharp a load of lies?

Keri: They weren't lies! We *did* find the lump of stone. And my dad *is* making a rockery in our back garden.

Ash: But you're not really going to take the stone home with you, are you?

Keri: No! You and I and this lump of stone are staying right here. Throw a different stone back in the river, We're going to wait and see if those people come back to look for their stone. There's something funny going on – and we're going to find out what it is!

Quiz

Play detective

- **p23** What is Ash about to tell Mr Sharp?
- **p24** Why does Keri elbow Ash in the ribs?
- **p25** What are the clues that Keri is clever at hiding the truth?
- **p25** Why does Keri say 'Um' when she answers Mr Sharp?
- **p26** What typical teacher instruction does Mr Sharp give Ash and Keri?
- **p26** Which one word sentence shows Keri is glad Mr Sharp has walked off?

Before reading
What It's Meant To Be

Setting the scene

Have you ever looked at an abstract painting and tried to decide what it reminds you of? Each person sees something different in an abstract painting.

Poem top tip

When you read the poem, make verse 2 sound exciting, verse 3 sound jokey, and verse 5 sound dreamy to convey the different effects the painting has on each person.

Quiz

Poem detective

- Why do you think the poet has used the informal language: Me and Dad and Gran?
- Why is the metaphor 'painting the night sky' effective?
- What do you think Gran thinks about the painting?

What It's Meant To Be

Me and Dad and Gran are in a gallery,
looking at a painting,
wondering what it's meant to be.

Dad says it looks like
fireworks painting the night
with fire.

Gran says it looks like
someone threw paint at the paper
and danced on it.

Me and Dad and Gran are in a gallery,
looking at a painting,
wondering what it's meant to be.

To me it looks like
what I see
in the night
when I dream.

by David Grant

Before reading
Art Surprises

Find out about

- Artwork made of unusual things such as toast or toy bricks
- Artwork that can be viewed either way up
- A blind painter

Tricky words

p31	sculptures	**p34**	studio
p32	exhibition	**p34**	chisel
p32	scraped	**p38**	plasticine

Text starter

Artists can make pictures and sculptures from all sorts of things. Emma Green made a picture out of toast and Nathan Sawaya makes sculptures out of toy bricks. The cartoonist, Gustave Verbeek, drew pictures that can work both the right way up and upside-down. Sargy Mann is a painter who is blind.

Art Surprises

Good Enough to Eat

Artist Prudence Emma Staite makes sculptures and pictures from all sorts of food. Her favourite food to work with is chocolate – she even makes chocolate skulls!

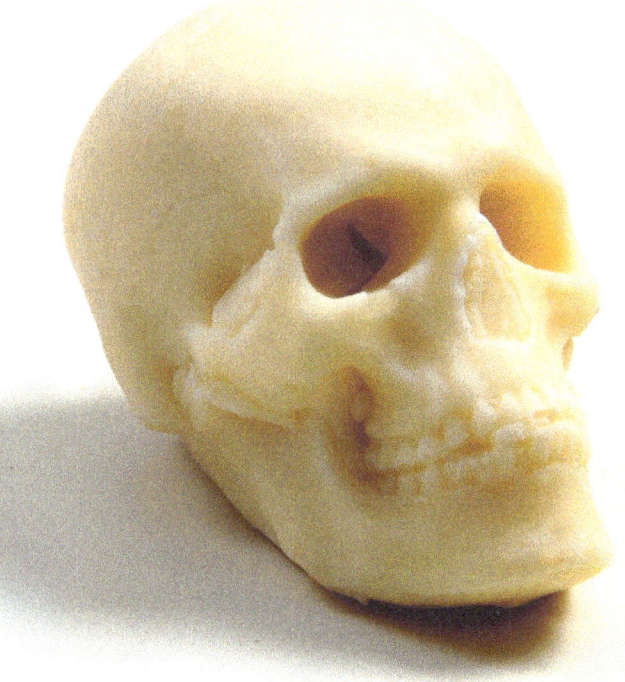

144 Things to do with Toast

When artist and sculptor Emma Green was asked to make a picture for an exhibition, she decided to re-create the painting of *Mona Lisa* … but she didn't use paint. She used toast!

First, she made the toast using slices of white bread. Then she glued the toast to a sheet of hardboard. Next, she scraped the toast to make the light and dark areas. She had to use a blow torch to create the black areas around the body.

It took three days to get the picture right, and it made Emma's house stink of toast! The picture was 180 cm by 70 cm, and Emma used 144 slices of bread.

Making Sculptures with Toy Bricks

Nathan Sawaya makes sculptures out of toy bricks. He has about 2.5 million bricks in his studio.

First, he sketches his ideas, and he uses a computer to help him work out the scale of his sculptures. Then he glues the bricks to each other as he works. If he makes a mistake he has to use a hammer and chisel to break the bricks apart.

The smallest thing he has made out of bricks is a tree – using one brown brick with one green brick on top! The largest thing he has made is a T-rex skeleton. It is 6 m long and made of 80 000 bricks. If he makes a life-sized human sculpture he uses around 15 000–25 000 bricks and it takes him 2–3 weeks to make it.

Upside-Down

Gustave Verbeek was a cartoonist and painter who worked in New York from around 1900. Verbeek created upside-down comic strips about the characters Lovekins and Mufaroo.

First, you read the strip one way, then you turn the comic upside-down and read the rest of the strip the other way. Each picture works the right way up and upside-down!

Look at the pictures. In the first one, Mufaroo is by an island, in a canoe which is being attacked by a big fish. When you look at the picture upside-down, you see a big bird with Lovekins in its beak.

5 Just as he reaches a small grassy point of land, another fish attacks him, lashing furiously with his tail.

8 The largest of the Rocs picks her up by the skirt.

Painting Blind

Sargy Mann is blind but he paints pictures of people and places he visited before he went blind. When he went blind, he had to find new ways to paint. He puts small pieces of plasticine on the canvas to help him feel his way around as he paints the picture. Sargy says that he 'feels' the colours as they go on the canvas.

Quiz

Text detective

- **p31** What might people be tempted to do with Prudence Emma Staite's sculptures?
- **p33** Why did Emma Green's house stink of toast?
- **p35** Do you think Nathan Sawaya's tree was a piece of artwork?
- **p36** What is surprising about Gustave Verbeek's cartoons?

Non-fiction features

- **p35** Think of a caption for this image.
- **p38** Why is the word 'feels' in inverted commas?

What do you think?

Why do artists experiment with pictures and sculptures made of all sorts of different things? Why would people pay a lot of money for a sculpture made of toy bricks? Can art be made out of anything?

HA! HA!

Q: Where do artists keep their clothes?

A: In draw-ers!

Published by Pearson Education Limited, a company incorporated in England and Wales, having its registered office at Edinburgh Gate, Harlow, Essex, CM20 2JE.
Registered company number: 872828

www.pearsonschools.co.uk

Pearson is a registered trademark of Pearson plc

Text © Pearson Education Limited 2013

The right of David Grant to be identified as the author of this work has been asserted by him in accordance with the Copyright, Designs and Patents Act 1988.

First published 2013

22
13

British Library Cataloguing in Publication Data is available from the British Library on request.

ISBN: 978 0 435 15242 0

Copyright notice
All rights reserved. No part of this publication may be reproduced in any form or by any means (including photocopying or storing it in any medium by electronic means and whether or not transiently or incidentally to some other use of this publication) without the written permission of the copyright owner, except in accordance with the provisions of the Copyright, Designs and Patents Act 1988 or under the terms of a licence issued by the Copyright Licensing agency, Saffron House, 6–10 Kirby Street, London EC1N 8TS (www.cla.co.uk). Applications for the copyright owner's written permission should be addressed to the publisher.

Designed by Bigtop
Original illustrations © Pearson Education Limited 2013
Illustrated by Rosy Higgins
Printed and bound in Great Britain by Ashford Colour Press Ltd.
Font © Pearson Education Ltd
Teaching notes by Dee Reid

Acknowledgements
We would like to thank the following schools for their invaluable help in the development and trialling of this course:
Callicroft Primary School, Bristol; Castlehill Primary School, Fife; Elmlea Junior School, Bristol; Lancaster School, Essex; Llanidloes School, Powys; Moulton School, Newmarket; Platt C of E Primary School, Kent; Sherborne Abbey CE VC Primary School, Dorset; Upton Junior School, Poole; Whitmore Park School, Coventry.

The publisher would like to thank the following for their kind permission to reproduce their photographs:

(Key: b-bottom; c-centre; l-left; r-right; t-top)

Food is Art Ltd: Prudence Emma Staite 31; **Nathan Sawaya:** 35; **Peter Mann:** 38; **Press Association Images:** Rui Vieira 33; **Veer/Corbis:** Ateli 29

All other images © Pearson Education

Every effort has been made to trace the copyright holders and we apologise in advance for any unintentional omissions. We would be pleased to insert the appropriate acknowledgement in any subsequent edition of this publication.